Newbridge Discovery Links®

MUD BUILDERS

Meish Goldish

Newbridge

A Haights Cross Communications Company

Mud Builders
ISBN: 1-4007-3659-5

Program Author: Dr. Brenda Parkes, Literacy Expert
Content Reviewer: Dr. Don Kaufman, Professor of Zoology,
Miami University, Oxford, OH

Written by Meish Goldish
Design Assistance by Kirchoff/Wohlberg, Inc.

Newbridge Educational Publishing
333 East 38th Street, New York, NY 10016
www.newbridgeonline.com

Cover Photograph: A beaver building a dam
Table of Contents Photograph: Nests made by potter wasps

Photo Credits
Cover: SuperStock; Table of Contents page: Noble Proctor/Photo Researchers; page 4: Leonard Lee Rue III/Photo Researchers; page 5: Brian Yarvin/Photo Researchers; page 6: Carl & Ann Purcell/Corbis; page 7: Peter Johnson/Corbis; page 9: Otto Lang/Corbis; page 10: (left) Kevin Schafer/Corbis, (right) Peter Ward/Bruce Coleman Inc.; page 11: Larry Harwood; page 12: Ken G. Preston-Mafham/Animals Animals; page 13: V.E. Ward/Photo Researchers; page 15: Dr. John Brackenbury/SPL/Photo Researchers; page 16: James L. Amos/Corbis; page 17: A. Morris/Vireo; page 19: Tom Bean/Corbis; page 20: Alan & Sandy Carey/Photo Researchers; page 21: Jack Wilburn/Animals Animals; page 22: G. Alan Nelson/Dembinsky Photo Associates; page 24: Dominique Braud/Animals Animals; page 25: Charlie Ott/Photo Researchers, (inset) Len Rue Jr./Photo Researchers; page 26: Neil Rabinowitz/Corbis; page 27: Paddy Ryan/Animals Animals; page 28: Neil Rabinowitz/Corbis; page 30: (from left to right) Otto Lang/Corbis, Tom Bean/Corbis, Neil Rabinowitz/Corbis, V.E. Ward/Photo Researchers, G. Alan Nelson/Dembinsky Photo Associates

Illustrations on pages 8, 14, 18, 23, 29 by Mike DiGiorgio

10 9 8 7 6 5 4 3 2 1

LEVEL
P

Table of Contents

AMAZING MUD

A flamingo builds its nest with mud. The cup-shaped top keeps eggs from rolling off.

Humans are not the only builders. Many kinds of animals build homes and other **structures**. Birds build cozy nests out of grass and twigs. Bees make wax to shape their hives.

Many animals build with one of the most useful of all materials—mud. In wet or rainy areas, mud is easy to find. In drier regions, animals make their own mud by mixing soil with water or their own **saliva**.

Are you surprised that animals build with mud? Don't be. Mud is an amazing material. For hundreds of years, Pueblo Indians in North America have lived in adobe houses. Adobe is really mud—a mixture of earth and water that gets hard when it dries. Adobe homes are suited to hot climates, because they stay cool inside.

Animals, too, use mud for building in ways that suit each creature's special needs.

Some adobe homes are built of sun-dried adobe bricks and covered with a smooth layer of mud.

A GIANT PILE-UP

This mud tower was built by termites that are only about the size of a pencil eraser!

Termites are among the world's smallest creatures. Yet in Africa and Australia, termites build the tallest animal homes on earth. A termite tower, called a **termitary**, may reach 8 meters high. That's much taller than a giraffe!

How do these tiny, antlike insects manage to create such gigantic homes? All it takes is teamwork, time, and lots of mud!

The process of building a termite tower starts with just two termites, a king and queen. They dig a hole in the ground about 30 centimeters deep. After mating, the queen begins to lay her eggs. That's her only job. The queen lays thousands of eggs a day for most of her life. Over time, millions of termites are born.

Most of the newborn termites are workers who build the termitary. Other termites are soldiers who guard the queen and the tower.

A queen is filled with so many eggs that she's unable to move about. She depends on workers to feed and care for her.

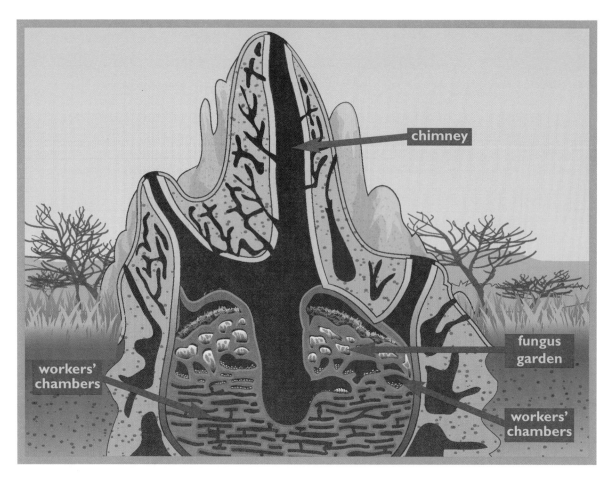

The king and queen live in the largest chamber in the termitary. In another space, the workers store food and take care of the eggs. Towers also have gardens of **fungus** that the termites eat.

Workers make mud by mixing soil with their own saliva or with water they suck from the earth. Then they begin building upward. As the mud rises, it hardens into a solid wall. The workers create a **network** of connecting tunnels and **chambers**, or rooms, inside the tower.

Even in hot climates, a termitary stays cool and comfortable inside. The hardened walls—about 50 centimeters thick—help to keep out heat. Cool air travels through the tunnels. Tiny holes in the walls allow stale air to escape and fresh air to enter.

chimney

A termite tower is totally dark inside. It doesn't bother the workers, though, since many have no eyes.

Termites build their tower with chimneys from which hot air can escape.

A termite tower is not built overnight. The job can take 10 to 50 years to complete. Since workers live only a few years, newborn workers carry on the task until the tower is finally finished. King and queen termites, however, may live up to 70 years. A mud termitary, once completed, can last a hundred years or more.

In rainy areas, termites build a mud mound with an umbrella-shaped roof. The roof protects the mound from rain.

This termite tower in New Mexico is believed to be millions of years old.

There are even some termite towers that have lasted for longer than 100 years. Recently, a team of scientists led by Stephen Hasiotis discovered ancient termitaries near Gallup, New Mexico. At first they thought the towers were just rock formations. The termites that live in North America today don't build towers. But when the scientists looked inside, they saw termite tunnels and chambers.

Hasiotis claims the towers date back between 135 and 195 million years ago. The termites that built them are long gone, but the termitaries are still here. That shows just how tough mud can be!

INCREDIBLE POTTERS!

A potter wasp forms its nest with tiny balls of mud.

Potter wasps, like termites, are insects that spend their lives building with mud. Potter wasps are named that because their nests are shaped like little clay pots.

Potter wasps build in a much different way than termites. For one thing, while termites are **social** insects that live in **colonies**, potters live and work alone.

Also, potters don't build homes for themselves, as termites do. Instead, they create nests for the eggs they lay.

When it comes to building a nest, the female potter wasp does all the work. She makes mud in a fascinating way. First she sucks up water to store in her stomach. Then she places grains of dry soil between her legs. Carefully, the potter spits water drops onto the soil. She rolls and rubs the mud with her legs until it is soft and sticky enough to work with.

The opening of a potter's nest is so narrow that even the mother cannot fit inside.

With fresh-made mud, the potter wasp can now start to build. Usually she picks a bush, tree twig, or crack in a rock as her nesting spot.

The potter wasp begins to shape the nest. She presses tiny mud balls together to form the outside. When it is finished, the entire nest is only about a centimeter wide. That's definitely smaller than a termite tower!

The potter wasp hunts and catches caterpillars and the **larvae** of beetles or other insects. She lines the bottom of

The potter wasp will stock her nest with up to 20 caterpillars for the wasp larva to eat.

egg

larva

A potter wasp nest is only about as wide as a fingernail.

A busy potter wasp makes separate trips to fly each mud ball to the nest.

her nest with them. Then she lays her egg and hangs it over the larvae from a sticky thread that she spins. She plugs the pot opening with mud to keep enemies out. After the egg hatches, the potter wasp larva eats the insect larvae beneath it. When it becomes an adult, it makes a hole in the side of the pot to fly out.

Meanwhile, the female potter wasp continues to work hard. She makes more mud and builds more nests for more eggs. In the world of potter wasps, a mother's work is never done. Or, you might say that a "mudder's" work is never done!

SNUG IN A JUG

Cliff swallows are social animals who live together in large colonies.

re insects like termites and potter wasps the only creatures that build with mud? Hardly! Among birds, cliff swallows are talented mud builders. They often make their nests on tall cliffs. The nests look like mud jugs.

You can find dozens—even hundreds—of swallow nests together on a single cliff. A cliff is a safe spot for the birds to lay their eggs and raise their babies. Most enemies can't get to such a high place.

A cliff swallow works hard to build a nest. It scoops a beakful of mud from a stream and flies it up to the cliff. Along the way, the bird shapes the mud into a small ball in its beak. The swallow returns again and again for more mud. One nest needs about 1,200 mud balls in all.

A cliff swallow keeps its wings and tail clean as it gathers mud.

The swallow begins making its nest by pressing a row of mud balls against a cliff. The mud balls stick to the cliff and serve as the base. Then the swallow adds layers of mud to shape the floor and walls. The bird leaves a small hole to enter and exit the nest.

A cliff swallow is careful while building its nest. Each layer of the nest must dry before the next layer can be added. It takes the bird a week or more to finish the entire home. It's worth the wait, however. A cliff swallow nest can last for several years.

mud balls

grasses and feathers

A cliff swallow nest is similar to a potter wasp nest, only much larger.

Cliff swallows often compete with one another for nests and eggs.

Despite their name, cliff swallows also build nests under bridges and inside barns.

In some places, thousands of cliff swallows live side by side. You might think the birds would get along well together. That is not always the case.

Biology professors Charles R. Brown and Mary Bomberger Brown studied large groups of cliff swallows in Nebraska to learn how they get along. They observed that the birds often fight among each other, especially when one swallow invades another's nest to steal or destroy its eggs. The fighting isn't pretty. When the mud starts flying, it's best to get out of the way!

STICKS IN THE MUD

A beaver uses its sharp teeth to cut the wood it needs to build a home.

eavers are known as skilled builders. The phrase "busy as a beaver" tells you how hard this mammal works to create a safe, comfortable home. Many people know that beavers build with wood such as tree logs and branches. What they may not realize is that beavers also build with mud.

Beavers create a home in two stages. First they build a dam in a river or stream. The dam stops the water from flowing, causing a pond to form. Then the beavers build their home. A beaver's home is called a **lodge**.

A beaver dam stretches across a river or stream and may be from 4 to 29 meters long. Often a whole family of beavers works together to build the wide dam out of sticks.

Beavers start by placing mud and rocks at the base of the dam. They get the mud from the bottom of the river or stream. They carry it by holding it against their chests with their front paws.

A beaver family, the male and female and their offspring, work together to build a dam.

Mud is important to beavers for another reason besides building. A beaver marks its territory with small mud piles. The mud carries the animal's scent. It tells other beavers, "Keep away!"

Beavers are known for their fast work. They are among nature's finest engineers.

The beavers then push rows of branches and sticks into the mud. Later, they pack on more mud so water can't seep through any cracks in the dam.

After a few days of busy building, the dam is completed. Whenever the dam needs repairs, the beavers quickly patch it with more mud. A well-kept dam can last for as many as 30 years.

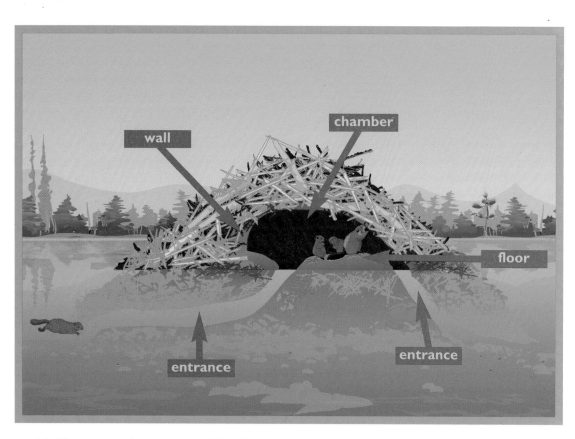

Unlike a termite tower, which has many small rooms, a beaver lodge has only one large chamber inside.

With the dam in place, the beavers can now build their lodge behind it, where a pond of calm water has formed. The family uses the same materials as for the dam. They place mud and rocks at the base of the lodge. Then they pile on sticks, twigs, and mud to shape the lodge like a tent or igloo. The lodge usually rises 1 to 2 meters above the water. The walls may be as thick as 1 meter.

A beaver lodge has one large chamber where the whole beaver family lives. The chamber floor sits about 15 centimeters above water level, so the beavers stay dry there.

A beaver's lodge has several underwater passages. Some of them are tunnels that lead from the chamber to the bottom of the pond. Beavers can use these tunnels to get in and out of the lodge quickly and easily. **Predators** such as wolves, however, cannot get into the lodge, because they generally will not go under water.

The tunnels also lead to a food supply of logs and branches stored near the base of the lodge. In winter, beavers swim under the ice to eat the bark.

Beavers are excellent swimmers. They can stay underwater for 4 to 5 minutes at a time.

The pond that forms when beavers dam up a river or stream is home to many fish and water birds.

For years, people have wondered whether beavers do more harm than good. They seem to cause much damage. They chew down many trees and clog the flow of rivers and streams.

However, scientists agree that beavers help nature in important ways. Muddy beaver dams keep soil from the river and stream banks from being washed away. The ponds that form when beaver dams are built may eventually turn into **wetlands** with many different kinds of plants and animals.

A mudskipper gets its name because it can skip, or skim, over mud and over the surface of water.

O f all animal mud builders, the mudskipper is among the strangest. This fish digs straight down into fresh mud along a seashore to make its **burrow**. The burrow is built mostly to protect the eggs that the female mudskipper lays. The mudskipper also uses its burrow to escape from its enemies.

How does this fish dig, having no arms or legs? Simple. When the tide is low, it scoops up mouthfuls of mud. It spits out each mouthful away from the burrow opening. The fish may burrow as deeply as one meter. That's a lot of mud in the mouth!

Mud is also important to mudskippers when they mate. The male attracts a female by doing a wild dance in the mud. He flops around on his belly and wiggles his fins. It's a messy way to get a partner, but it works!

The male then brings the female into his burrow. The burrow, of course, has water in it. It also has air in it. The female lays her eggs in the burrow. Either the male or female watches the eggs until they hatch two or three weeks later.

One type of mudskipper can climb up rocks, roots, and trees. It uses its strong fins to pull itself upward.

Scientists have long been fascinated by the mudskipper. That's because it is one of the few fish that can live and breathe on land. At low tide, you'll often find the mudskipper using its fins to "walk" along the mud.

Mudskippers can move faster when they are "skipping" across the mud or the water's surface than when they are swimming.

How is it possible for the mudskipper to breathe both underwater and on land? Just like other fish, the mudskipper has **gills** for breathing underwater. When the mudskipper is on land, it breathes in two different ways. It breathes through its gills, getting oxygen from water it stores up in its body. It also breathes by absorbing oxygen through the lining of its mouth and throat and through its skin.

The mudskipper is a marine fish. That means it lives in salt water.

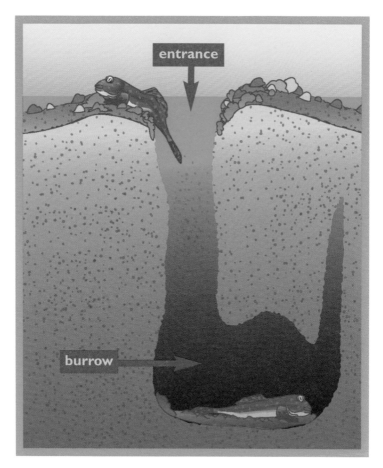

Mudskippers' burrows can be more than one meter deep. There's usually a pool of water covering the entrance of the burrow.

entrance

burrow

Recently, researchers from Nagasaki University, led by Atsushi Ishimatsu, studied mudskipper burrows in Malaysia. To their surprise, they found that the deep mud home of a mudskipper contains a large amount of air.

By observing mudskippers, they discovered how the air got there. They saw mudskippers swallowing air just before entering their burrows. When they left the burrows, the fish looked flatter. The scientists realized that the mudskippers themselves were supplying the air they need to breathe while they are in their burrows.

AT HOME IN THE MUD

potter wasp pot

termite tower

cliff swallow jugs

mudskipper burrow

beaver dam

Animals build mud homes in their own ways to meet their individual needs.

When you think about the material you would use to build your dream home, mud may not be the first thing that comes to mind. But for many creatures, mud is the perfect building material.

What's so great about mud? If termites could talk, they'd tell you that it's long-lasting and keeps a room cool. Potter wasps would say that mud holds its shape, and cliff swallows would say that mud sticks well to surfaces. Beavers would tell you that it's great for plugging cracks and holding sticks together. And a mudskipper would praise mud as something great to dig into.

All would agree: There's no place like a mud home!

GLOSSARY

burrow: an underground tunnel or hole an animal uses as its home

chamber: a large room or space

colony: a group of animals that live together

fungus: a type of plantlike organism; mushrooms and mold are both fungi

gill: the organ fish use for breathing

larva: wormlike creature that hatches from an insect egg

lodge: a shelter or home

network: a series or system of connected tunnels, rivers, or other things

predator: an animal that hunts or eats other animals

saliva: a clear liquid formed in the mouth of an animal

social: living together in a group or community

structure: a building or other object that has been built

termitary: the nest or tower where termites live

wetlands: an area of land where the soil is always wet

Index

Websites

www.oaklandzoo.org/atoz/atoz.html
www.sandiegozoo.org/wildideas/kids/index.html